Holiday Fun

Seasonal Starters 🍃

Roasted Red Pepper Dip

  1 (8-ounce) container sour cream
  1 (7-ounce) jar roasted red peppers, drained
  4 ounces cream cheese
  ½ teaspoon chopped fresh or frozen chives
    Fresh chives, for garnish
    WHEAT THINS Snack Crackers

1. Blend sour cream, peppers, cream cheese and chopped chives with blender or electric mixer until well mixed.

2. Spoon into bowl; refrigerate for at least 1 hour.

3. Garnish with chives if desired. Serve as dip with snack crackers.   *Makes 2 cups*

Preparation Time: 15 minutes
Chill Time: 1 hour
Total Time: 1 hour and 15 minutes

Roasted Red Pepper Dip

Wisconsin Wings

18 RITZ Crackers, finely crushed (about ¾ cup crumbs)
⅓ cup grated Parmesan cheese
1 teaspoon dried oregano leaves
½ teaspoon garlic powder
½ teaspoon paprika
⅛ teaspoon coarse ground black pepper
2 pounds chicken wings, split and tips removed
⅓ cup GREY POUPON Dijon Mustard

1. Mix cracker crumbs, Parmesan cheese, oregano, garlic powder, paprika and pepper in shallow dish; set aside.

2. Coat chicken wing pieces with mustard; roll in crumb mixture to coat. Place on greased baking sheet.

3. Bake at 350°F for 35 to 40 minutes or until golden brown, turning pieces over halfway through baking time. Serve warm.

Makes 12 servings

Preparation Time: 25 minutes
Cook Time: 35 minutes
Total Time: 1 hour

Holiday Fundamentals

Crush crackers quickly and easily by placing them in a sealed plastic food storage bag, then running a rolling pin over the bag several times to pulverize them.

Brie Amandine

24 TRISCUIT Wafers
4 ounces Brie, cut into 24 small wedges
¼ cup apricot preserves
PLANTERS Sliced Almonds

1. Top each wafer with 1 piece of cheese, ½ teaspoon preserves and sliced almonds. Place on baking sheet.

2. Bake at 350°F for 2 to 3 minutes or until cheese melts.

Makes 24 servings

Preparation Time: 20 minutes
Cook Time: 2 minutes
Total Time: 22 minutes

Horseradish Bacon Dip

2 cups shredded Cheddar cheese (8 ounces)
1 cup sour cream
¼ cup crumbled, cooked bacon (about 2 strips)
1 tablespoon prepared horseradish
2 tablespoons chopped chives
WHEAT THINS Snack Crackers

1. Blend cheese, sour cream, bacon and horseradish in blender or food processor. Stir in chives. Refrigerate for at least 1 hour to blend flavors.

2. Serve as spread with snack crackers.

Makes 1½ cups

Preparation Time: 15 minutes
Chill Time: 1 hour
Total Time: 1 hour and 15 minutes

Brie Amandine

Deviled Vegetable Crab Spread

1 (8-ounce) package cream cheese, softened
¼ cup GREY POUPON Dijon Mustard
2 tablespoons milk
12 PREMIUM Crackers (any variety), finely crushed (½ cup crumbs)
1 (6-ounce) can crabmeat or tuna, drained and flaked
¼ cup chopped green onions
¼ cup chopped red bell pepper
Additional PREMIUM Crackers

1. Beat cream cheese in small bowl with electric mixer at medium speed until smooth; add mustard and milk, beating until well blended.

2. Add cracker crumbs, crabmeat or tuna, green onions and bell pepper. Place in greased 8-inch pie plate or small baking dish.

3. Bake at 350°F for 20 minutes or until golden brown and hot. Serve as a spread with crackers.   *Makes about 2⅓ cups*

Preparation Time: 30 minutes
Cook Time: 20 minutes
Total Time: 50 minutes

For more holiday recipes and crafts, visit us at **nabiscorecipes.com.**

Sundried Tomato Cheese Puffs

24 RITZ Crackers
1 cup shredded mozzarella cheese (4 ounces)
¼ cup chopped drained oil-packed sundried tomatoes
4 eggs, beaten
¾ cup milk
2 tablespoons chopped fresh parsley
1 tablespoon chopped fresh basil or 1 teaspoon dried basil leaves
2 tablespoons grated Parmesan cheese

1. Place 2 crackers in each of 12 lightly greased 2½-inch muffin-pan cups; evenly top with mozzarella cheese and tomatoes.

2. Blend eggs, milk, parsley and basil. Pour evenly over cheese layer; sprinkle with Parmesan cheese.

3. Bake at 350°F for 30 to 35 minutes or until puffed and golden brown. Let stand 5 minutes. Loosen edges and remove from pan. Serve warm. *Makes 12 appetizers*

Preparation Time: 25 minutes
Cook Time: 30 minutes
Cooling Time: 5 minutes
Total Time: 1 hour

Cheesy Stuffed Eggs

    6 hard-cooked eggs
    ¼ cup EASY CHEESE Sharp Cheddar Pasteurized
        Process Cheese Spread
    2 tablespoons mayonnaise
    2 tablespoons GREY POUPON Dijon Mustard
    2 tablespoons finely chopped parsley
        EASY CHEESE Pasteurized Process Cheese Spread,
        for garnish
        Chopped pimientos, for garnish

1. Halve eggs lengthwise. Scoop yolks into bowl; set egg
white halves aside.

2. Mash yolks; blend in cheese spread, mayonnaise, mustard
and parsley. Spoon or pipe mixture into egg white halves.
Cover; refrigerate until serving time.

3. Serve topped with additional cheese spread and pimientos
if desired.   *Makes 12 appetizers*

Preparation Time: 30 minutes
Total Time: 30 minutes

Cheddar Beer Dip

    1 (8-ounce) package cream cheese, softened
    ½ cup beer
    2 cups shredded sharp Cheddar cheese (8 ounces)
        WHEAT THINS Snack Crackers

1. Beat cream cheese in medium bowl with electric mixer until
smooth; gradually blend in beer. Add Cheddar cheese,
beating until well blended.

2. Refrigerate until serving time. Serve as dip with snack
crackers.   *Makes about 2½ cups*

Preparation Time: 15 minutes
Total Time: 15 minutes

Cheesy Stuffed Eggs

Ham Pinwheels

1 (8-ounce) package cream cheese, softened
4 (1/16-inch-thick) slices boiled ham
4 teaspoons snipped fresh or frozen chives
    RITZ Crackers

1. Spread 1/4 cup cream cheese to edges on each ham slice; sprinkle each with 1 teaspoon chives.

2. Beginning at short end, roll up tightly. Wrap and refrigerate ham rolls at least 2 hours.

3. Cut each roll crosswise into 10 slices. Place 1 slice on each cracker. Serve immediately.   *Makes 40 appetizers*

Preparation Time: 30 minutes
Chill Time: 2 hours
Total Time: 2 hours and 30 minutes

Blue Cheese and Bacon Dip

1 cup sour cream
8 ounces sliced bacon, cooked and crumbled
4 ounces crumbled blue cheese
1 (6.5-ounce) package STELLA D'ORO Snack Stix, any flavor

1. Mix sour cream, bacon and blue cheese in bowl. Refrigerate at least 1 hour to blend flavors.

2. Serve as dip with snack sticks.   *Makes 2 cups dip*

Preparation Time: 15 minutes
Chill Time: 1 hour
Total Time: 1 hour and 15 minutes

Ham Pinwheels

Spinach Dip

1 (16-ounce) container sour cream
1 (10-ounce) package frozen chopped spinach,
    thawed and well drained
¼ cup chopped red bell pepper
¼ cup chopped green onions
1 clove garlic, crushed
½ teaspoon liquid hot pepper seasoning
    WHEAT THINS Snack Crackers

1. Blend sour cream, spinach, bell pepper, green onions, garlic and pepper seasoning in bowl. Cover; refrigerate at least 1 hour to blend flavors.

2. Serve as dip with snack crackers.   *Makes 2 cups*

Preparation Time: 10 minutes
Chill Time: 1 hour
Total Time: 1 hour and 10 minutes

Pecan Cheese Ball

1 (8-ounce) package cream cheese, softened
1 cup shredded Cheddar cheese (4 ounces)
½ cup crumbled blue cheese (4 ounces)
½ cup PLANTERS Pecans, chopped
    RITZ Crackers

1. Blend cheeses in medium bowl with electric mixer at medium speed.

2. Shape cheese mixture into ball; roll in pecans. Refrigerate for at least 1 hour.

3. Serve as spread with crackers.   *Makes 2 cups spread*

Preparation Time: 15 minutes
Chill Time: 1 hour
Total Time: 1 hour and 15 minutes

Spinach Dip

Cheesy Quiche Bites

36 RITZ Crackers, finely crushed (about 1½ cups crumbs)
3 tablespoons margarine or butter, melted
2 cups shredded Cheddar cheese (8 ounces)
½ cup chopped roasted red peppers
4 eggs, beaten
¾ cup milk
½ cup GREY POUPON Dijon or COUNTRY DIJON Mustard
¼ cup chopped fresh parsley
¼ cup grated Parmesan cheese

1. Mix cracker crumbs and margarine or butter; press on bottom of greased 13×9×2-inch pan. Bake at 350°F for 8 to 10 minutes or until golden. Remove from oven; let stand for 5 minutes.

2. Sprinkle half the Cheddar cheese over crust; top with peppers and remaining Cheddar cheese.

3. Blend eggs, milk, mustard and parsley in small bowl; pour evenly over cheese in prepared pan. Sprinkle with Parmesan cheese. Bake at 350°F for 30 to 35 minutes or until set. Let stand 10 minutes; cut into 2×1½-inch bars. Serve warm.

Makes 32 appetizers

Preparation Time: 30 minutes
Cook Time: 38 minutes
Total Time: 1 hour and 8 minutes

Shrimp Cocktail Spread

- **1 envelope KNOX Unflavored Gelatine**
- **½ cup skim milk**
- **3 (4-ounce) cans baby shrimp, drained**
- **1 cup prepared cocktail sauce**
- **1 cup sour cream**
- **2 tablespoons prepared horseradish**
- **⅓ cup chopped green onions**
  RITZ Crackers

1. Sprinkle gelatine over skim milk in small saucepan; let stand 1 minute. Stir gelatine over low heat until completely dissolved, about 3 minutes. Set aside.

2. Blend shrimp, cocktail sauce, sour cream and horseradish in food processor until smooth. Gradually add gelatine mixture until well blended. Stir in green onions.

3. Pour mixture into 4-cup mold. Refrigerate at least 4 hours or until firm.

4. Unmold onto serving dish; serve as spread with crackers.

Makes 4 cups spread

Preparation Time: 25 minutes
Cook Time: 3 minutes
Chill Time: 4 hours
Total Time: 4 hours and 28 minutes

For more holiday recipes and crafts, visit us at **nabiscorecipes.com.**

Holiday Houses & Crafts

Graham Cracker House

9 squares HONEY MAID Honey Grahams
½ cup prepared white frosting
9 Mini OREO Chocolate Sandwich Cookies
Assorted cookies, crackers and candies, for garnish

1. Using 1 cracker for floor and 4 for walls, assemble house, sealing all seams with frosting. Cut 1 cracker in half diagonally; with frosting, attach cut sides of cracker halves to opposite ends of house top to form roof supports. With frosting, attach 2 crackers to form roof, sealing all edges. Allow house to dry completely.

2. Cut remaining cracker to use for doors and windows; attach with frosting. Separate cookies. Attach to roof, filling-side down, with frosting. Decorate as desired using remaining frosting, cookies, crackers and candies.   *Makes 1 house*

Graham Cracker House

Festive Oreo Cookie Tree

1 cardboard party hat (7 inches high, 5-inch base)
  Plastic wrap
1 (9-inch) sturdy paper plate
1 cup prepared white frosting
18 Holiday OREO Chocolate Sandwich Cookies
  Assorted candies, colored gels and colored sugars
    for decorating

1. Cover party hat with plastic wrap. Secure party hat to paper plate using small amount of frosting; let dry 10 minutes.

2. Carefully separate each cookie, leaving red filling on one side; set cookie halves without filling aside. Decorate red filling side of remaining cookie halves using assorted candies, colored gels and sugars. Decorate 1 cookie with star.

3. Starting at base of party hat, alternately attach decorated and plain cookies to hat as pictured, using frosting. Allow cookies to dry on hat base in between rows. Top with star-decorated cookie. Use as decorative centerpiece.

Makes 1 tree

Holiday Fundamentals

Let your imagination run wild when you decorate this tree! Pipe simple designs such as snowflakes, Christmas trees, holly leaves and snowmen on some of the cookie halves. Or, pipe the names of your family and friends on the cookies to personalize the tree. Use colorful small candies to decorate the rest of the cookies—many supermarkets and craft stores carry holiday-colored and holiday-themed candies at this time of year.

Santa's Jalopy

- 11 whole (5×2½-inch) **HONEY MAID Honey Grahams**
  Royal Frosting (page 43)
- 1 stick **CARE*FREE Peppermint Gum**
- 1 thin pretzel stick
- 1 green **LIFE SAVERS Roll Candy**
- 4 Holiday **OREO Chocolate Sandwich Cookies**
- 1 stick **ICE BREAKERS Hot Cinnamon Gum**
- 2 sticks **FRUIT STRIPE Gum**
- 1 red **LIFE SAVERS Roll Candy**
- 2 yellow **LIFE SAVERS Roll Candies**
- 2 **TEDDY GRAHAMS Graham Snacks, any flavor**
  Red decorator icing
  Assorted decorated cookies and candies

1. Make car base: Cut 5 whole grahams crosswise in half to form 10 squares. Cut 6 whole grahams into 4 pieces along perforated lines to form 24 rectangles. Place one graham square, one graham rectangle and one graham square side by side on work surface. Trim sides of both graham squares so front and back of car base narrow to 1½ inches. Join side by side pieces with frosting.

2. Make car body: For car sides, lay 1 graham square, 1 graham rectangle and 1 graham square side by side. Trim top side of each graham square so front and back ends of car are 1¼ inches high. Stand pieces on end; attach side pieces together and attach bottom of side piece to car base using frosting. Repeat to make other side of car with 2 graham squares and 1 graham rectangle. Cut front grill and back of car from 2 graham rectangles; attach to car using frosting. Cut car hood from 1 graham square to fit; attach to car using frosting. Cut graham quarters and stack to fit inside car for front seat; secure with frosting. Cut peppermint gum for front windshield; attach with frosting. Insert pretzel stick into green roll candy for steering wheel and steering column; attach bottom of steering column to inside car base. Arrange

continued on page 24

Santa's Jalopy, continued

2 graham rectangles end to end on waxed paper; pipe a strip of frosting onto grahams. Set car on graham rectangles.

3. Decorate car: Attach chocolate sandwich cookies to car body for wheels with frosting. Cut cinnamon gum for fenders, headlight trim and running board; attach to car with frosting. Cut stripe gum for front and rear bumpers; attach to car with frosting. Using frosting with small star tip (#18), decorate car hood and body. Attach red roll candy using frosting for front hood ornament. Using frosting with small writing tip make front grill and decorate around door, fenders and wheel hubs. Attach yellow roll candies with frosting as headlights. Stand bear-shaped snacks on front seat. Use red icing to trim windshield and make door handle. Fill car with decorated cookie and candy "packages" as desired. *Makes 1 jalopy*

Holiday Fundamentals

If you'd like to add some scenery to your cookie crafts, start with a few easy trees. Simply pipe green-tinted frosting over inverted ice cream (sugar) cones, adding colored decorations if desired.

Oreo Express

- **4 whole (5×2½ inches) HONEY MAID Honey Grahams**
  Royal Frosting (page 43)
- **4 White Fudge Covered OREO Chocolate Sandwich**
  Cookies
- **1 Holiday Chunky CHIPS AHOY! Chocolate Chip Cookie**
- **6 Holiday OREO Chocolate Sandwich Cookies**
- **2 sticks FRUIT STRIPE Gum**
- **1 green LIFE SAVERS Roll Candy**
  Cotton, for smoke stack
- **1 yellow LIFE SAVERS Roll Candy**
- **1 green LIFE SAVERS GUMMI SAVERS CRYSTAL**
  CRAZE! Candy
- **2 red LIFE SAVERS Roll Candies**
- **2 Mini OREO Chocolate Sandwich Cookies**
  Green decorator icing

1. For engine base, cut off corners of end of 1 graham;
trim second graham to match. Spread thin layer of frosting
on top of 1 graham; top with second graham, pressing lightly
to sandwich. To make wheel supports, cut 2 grahams into
6 pieces that measure about 1½×¾ inches each. Using
frosting, stack 3 graham pieces together. Repeat with remaining
graham pieces to make second support. Fasten supports (like
wheel axles) on bottom of base.

2. For engine, stack 4 white fudge covered cookies with
frosting between cookies to form engine cab. Attach chocolate
chip cookie to top with frosting. Secure engine cab to engine
base with frosting as pictured. Stack 4 red-filled chocolate
sandwich cookies as for cab and stand on edge, attaching
to engine base with frosting in front of cab as pictured.

3. Wrap 1 stick gum in a circle for smoke stack. (If gum is
too stiff to roll, quickly run under hot water and dry thoroughly;
roll immediately.) Attach gum roll to front of engine with frosting
as pictured; secure green roll candy on top of smoke stack
with frosting. Attach small piece of cotton to top for smoke.

continued on page 26

Oreo Express, continued

4. Cut remaining 1 stick gum crosswise along length at ⅛-inch intervals, not cutting through to other side; fan slightly and attach to engine base front with frosting to form cattle guard. Sandwich 1 yellow roll candy and 1 gummi candy with frosting; attach to front of engine with frosting for headlight. Attach 2 red roll candies to remaining 2 red-filled chocolate sandwich cookies with frosting for rear engine wheels; attach to rear of engine. Attach 2 mini chocolate sandwich cookies with frosting for front wheels. Decorate engine as pictured using frosting and green decorator icing.

Makes 1 train

Holiday Fundamentals

With a variety of cookies and candies on hand, it's easy to create the perfect setting for your train. Kids can help out with this part of the project too: use sticks of gum and licorice to form train tracks in a snap; a combination of gum, pretzels and gum drops makes a colorful railroad crossing sign. Complete the scene with a few Marshmallow Snowmen (page 90) or several Teddy Graham snacks decorated as conductors.

Nabisco Holiday House

23 whole (5×2½-inch) HONEY MAID Honey Grahams
2 (16-ounce) cans white frosting
43 White Fudge Covered OREO Chocolate Sandwich
  Cookies
46 LIFE SAVERS Roll Candies (red and green)
13 LIFE SAVERS GUMMI SAVERS CRYSTAL CRAZE!
  Candies
2 sticks FRUIT STRIPE Gum
6 Holiday OREO Chocolate Sandwich Cookies, halved
24 NILLA Wafers
15 green gum drops
  Assorted color decorator icing

1. Construct base and frame for house as pictured, measuring 10×7½ inches, using stiff cardboard or foam core.

2. Attach 19 grahams to front and sides of house frame with some frosting, cutting grahams to fit. Attach 40 white fudge covered cookies to roof frame with frosting, overlapping as pictured. Decorate roof with frosting as pictured using pastry bag fitted with small star tip. Attach roll candy and gummi candy to roof as pictured.

3. Break remaining grahams along scoring into 4 (2½-inch×1¼-inch) rectangles. Attach to house for shutters as pictured. Attach gum pieces to house for front door. Halve remaining white fudge covered cookies and attach above windows as pictured. Place halved holiday chocolate sandwich cookies, wafers and gum drops around house as pictured, using halved wafers for front steps.

4. Use decorator icing to make wreaths, bows and pine boughs on house and decorate house as desired.

Makes 1 house

Jolly Snowman

2 White Fudge Covered OREO Chocolate Sandwich Cookies
Royal Frosting (page 43) or prepared white frosting
2 sticks FRUIT STRIPE Gum
Blue sugar sprinkles
1 semisweet chocolate chip
1 *each* red and yellow LIFE SAVERS Roll Candy
Red decorator icing

1. Attach 2 cookies with frosting to form snowman. Cut 1 end of 1 stick gum as "scarf" fringe and other end tapered to ⅜-inch wide. Wrap "scarf" around snowman's neck.

2. Cut 2 triangles from remaining 1 stick gum; attach to snowman for eyes with frosting. Using frosting, attach blue sugar in center of eyes, chocolate chip for nose and roll candies for buttons on body. With red icing, draw mouth on snowman. Let dry. *Makes 1 snowman*

Santa

1 Holiday Chunky CHIPS AHOY! Chocolate Chip Cookie
7 LIFE SAVERS Wint-O-Green Roll Candies
Royal Frosting (page 43) or prepared white frosting
1 red LIFE SAVERS Roll Candy
Red decorator icing
1 Holiday OREO Chocolate Sandwich Cookie

1. Select chocolate chip cookie with 2 chips in good positions for eyes. Place on waxed paper. Attach 6 mint candies to bottom of cookie with frosting using star tip to form beard.

2. Break off piece of red candy; attach with icing or frosting for nose. Draw mouth with red icing.

3. Split sandwich cookie, leaving icing on one side. Cut ¼-inch slice off filled side; attach to head to form hat as pictured.

4. Pipe frosting along bottom of hat, using star tip. Attach remaining mint candy at top. Let dry. *Makes 1 Santa*

Left to right: Jolly Snowmen and Santa

Cookie Castle

4 empty half-gallon cardboard milk cartons
Royal Frosting (page 43)
12 whole (5×2½-inch) HONEY MAID Honey Grahams
20 Holiday OREO Chocolate Sandwich Cookies
12 Holiday CHIPS AHOY! Chocolate Chip Cookies
27 pieces Ballistic Berry BUBBLE YUM Bubble Gum
2 COMET Sugar Cones
9 sticks CARE*FREE Peppermint Gum
Yellow food coloring
2 JET-PUFFED Miniature Marshmallows
1 stick FRUIT STRIPE Gum
1 package LIFE SAVERS Five Flavor Roll Candy
2 TEDDY GRAHAMS Graham Snacks, any flavor

1. Make castle frame: Rinse cartons. Using razor blade or mat knife, cut off tops of cartons 5¼ inches from bottom; discard tops. Turn cartons upside down and tape together to form square. Using frosting, attach 3 whole grahams to each of 3 sides of frame (corners of frame will show). Cut 1 whole graham in half to make 2 squares. On remaining side of frame, attach halved graham on right top (this will be over drawbridge door); place remaining whole grahams to left of halved graham. Cut out uncovered cardboard square to make drawbridge door opening.

2. Make castle columns: Stack 10 chocolate sandwich cookies, securing with 1 teaspoon frosting between cookies; repeat to make a second stack. Attach each column to right and left front corners of castle with frosting.

3. Make roof and floor: Spread frosting on castle roof; press 9 chocolate chip cookies into frosting. Spread frosting inside castle drawbridge door; press 3 cookies into frosting, cutting to fit. Halve 9 pieces of bubble gum; alternately attach whole and halved pieces of bubble gum along top edge of each side of castle. Stand ice cream cones, top-side down, on each column.

continued on page 34

Cookie Castle

Cookie Castle, continued

4. Make windows: Brush peppermint gum sticks with yellow food coloring, using damp paper towel to even the color. Cut each stick in half to form 18 pieces. For 3 front top windows, place 2 gum pieces side by side for each window; round the top corners. Attach three windows with frosting, evenly spacing across the top. Repeat for 3 windows across the back side of castle. Attach 3 single pieces of gum across each side of the castle.

5. Decorate: Using frosting and small writing tip, pipe trim between bubble gum on roof and make stripes up ice cream cones. Press marshmallows on points of ice cream cones. Attach remaining graham square for drawbridge door in down position. Cut gum into ⅛-inch strips and attach to door frame. Place roll candy in plastic bag and coarsely crush with rolling pin to ⅛- to ¼-inch pieces. Using frosting and small writing tip, pipe trim around 1 window and insert candy pieces to look like stone. Repeat for all windows and door. Stand bear-shaped graham snacks on drawbridge door.   *Makes 1 castle*

Holiday Fundamentals

Creating the Cookie Castle is more than child's play, but your kids can make great helpers. They'll love stacking the Oreos together with frosting to form the columns, and they can help build the roof with cookies and bubble gum. They can also use their artistic talents for decorating the windows and doors with crushed candies. And once the castle is complete, kids can add an army of Teddy Graham "guards" to protect the kingdom.

Triscuit Teddy House

5 TRISCUIT Wafers
  Royal Frosting (page 43) or prepared white frosting
  Green sugar sprinkles
1 TEDDY GRAHAMS Graham Snack
3 LIFE SAVERS Roll Candies, halved
  Ribbon

1. Attach long edges of 2 wafers with frosting to form roof; stand on edge on waxed paper.

2. For sides of house, attach short edges of 2 wafers to each side of roof as pictured on page 37. Attach 1 wafer for floor; let dry. Stand house upright.

3. Pipe icing or frosting onto floor of house and sprinkle with green sugar sprinkles. Stand bear-shaped graham snack in house and attach to floor with frosting.

4. Pipe icing or frosting at roof peak and attach 5 candy halves over peak. Decorate roof with frosting; let dry. To hang on tree, slip 10-inch piece of thin ribbon through house and tie into bow.

Makes 1 house

Bell Ornament

Royal Frosting (page 43)
1 ROYAL LUNCH Milk Cracker
2 White Fudge Covered OREO Chocolate Sandwich
   Cookies
1 NILLA Wafer
1 FARLEY'S Gummi Ring, any flavor
1 red LIFE SAVERS Roll Candy
Red or green food coloring
Colored sugar
1 JET-PUFFED Miniature Marshmallow

1. Stack ingredients in following order securing with frosting in between: milk cracker, 2 white fudge covered chocolate sandwich cookies, vanilla wafer and gummi ring.

2. Stand red roll candy in center of gummi ring at top of ornament securing with frosting. Tint some frosting with red or green food coloring if desired. Decoratively pipe tinted frosting on bell using star or writing tip; sprinkle with colored sugar. Let dry.

3. Thread ribbon through red roll candy and tie into bow to hang. Attach marshmallow to bottom of bell with frosting. Stand bell over glass with smaller opening than width of bell to let dry.   *Makes 1 ornament*

Bell Ornament and
Triscuit Teddy House (page 35)

Santa's Sleigh

1 stick FRUIT STRIPE Gum
1 square HONEY MAID Honey Graham
2 green LIFE SAVERS GUMMI SAVERS CRYSTAL
    CRAZE! Candies
Royal Frosting (page 43) or prepared white frosting
2 red LIFE SAVERS Roll Candies
Red decorator icing
FRUIT STRIPE Gum, assorted colors
1 TEDDY GRAHAMS Graham Snack

1. Cut 1 stick gum in half lengthwise to form 2 sleigh runners; curl ends around pencil for front of runners.

2. Cut graham in half along perforation. Cut one piece to 2¼-inch length and other piece to 1¼-inch length.

3. Cut gummi candies in half. Attach halved candies, cut sides down, to runners with frosting. Attach longer graham piece on top of candies for sleigh base.

4. Attach smaller graham piece at back end of sleigh base with frosting. Attach roll candies as shown. Decorate with frosting and red icing.

5. Cut assorted gum sticks into pieces for "packages;" decorate with icing for ribbons and bows. Let dry.

6. Arrange "packages" and bear-shaped graham snack in sleigh.   *Makes 1 sleigh*

For more holiday recipes and crafts, visit us at **nabiscorecipes.com.**

Candy Cane Cottage

    1 empty 2-quart cardboard milk or juice carton
   10 whole (5×2 ½ inches) HONEY MAID Honey Grahams
        Royal Frosting (page 43)
   20 red LIFE SAVERS Roll Candies
   20 individually wrapped LIFE SAVERS Candy Cane Roll
        Candies
    5 pieces FRUIT STRIPE Gum
    2 BISCOS Sugar Wafers
        Red decorator icing
    3 pieces Wild Strawberry BUBBLE YUM Bubble Gum
    1 TEDDY GRAHAMS Graham Snack

1. Make frame for house: Rinse carton and staple or tape
top closed. Cut 4 inches from bottom of carton; discard bottom
section. Place top portion on piece of waxed paper. Cut
6 grahams to height of 3¾ inches to form sides. Cut
2 of these pieces in half lengthwise along perforation. Using
frosting, attach 1 whole graham and 1 long piece to each side
of carton, making grahams even with bottom edge of carton
and centering on each side of carton. To form roof base,
attach 1 whole graham sideways at top ridge of carton using
frosting under graham to build to ridge height. Repeat for
other side of roof. Cut remaining grahams with serrated knife
to fit under eaves on sides of house.

2. Tile roof: Spread frosting generously on one side of roof.
Beginning at bottom, quickly press row of alternating red and
candy cane roll candies, allowing first row of candies to
overhang graham roof base. Continue rows to top, overlapping
each row slightly. Repeat for second side of roof.

continued on page 42

Candy Cane cottage, continued

3. Make windows: Cut 4 sticks gum into 7 (1¼-inch) pieces for windows; cut remaining stick gum into arched window above door 1½ inches long and ⅝ inch high at center. Attach windows to house with frosting.

4. Make door: Spread frosting thinly on back of 2 sugar wafers. Press side-by-side on waxed paper to form door. With red decorator icing using small petal or leaf tip, pipe ribbon on door to look like a gift box; top with bow made with frosting using same tip. Let dry. Peel from waxed paper and attach to house with frosting.

5. Make chimney and decorate house: For chimney top, cut out center of 1 piece bubble gum using sharp knife, leaving about ⅛-inch shell around outside edge. Using frosting to attach, stack three pieces of bubble gum ending with cut out piece
on top as pictured. With frosting using star tip, pipe border at corners of house and at peak of roof. Press chimney into place. With frosting using writing tip, draw window panes and outline windows and door with small beads. Pipe icicles around eaves and snow on the chimney top. Stand bear-shaped graham snack in chimney.

Holiday Fundamentals

To cut graham crackers into the right shapes and sizes for these houses and crafts, use a serrated knife and a gentle sawing motion. A straight-edge knife is more likely to break the grahams.

Royal Frosting

½ cup refrigerated pasteurized egg whites*
½ teaspoon cream of tartar
1 (16-ounce) box powdered sugar

*3 tablespoons meringue powder or 2 tablespoons egg white powder dissolved in 6 tablespoons warm water can be substituted for pasteurized egg whites. Dissolve according to package directions.

1. Beat egg whites and cream of tartar with mixer at high speed until blended.

2. Add powdered sugar on low speed until blended; beat on high speed about 5 minutes until stiff peaks form.

3. Cover icing at all times to prevent hardening. To store several hours or overnight, place plastic wrap directly on surface of icing; refrigerate. Beat with mixer until stiff before using.

Makes about 2½ cups

For more holiday recipes and crafts, visit us at
nabiscorecipes.com.

Heavenly Angel

1 White Fudge Covered OREO Chocolate Sandwich
   Cookie
2 individually wrapped LIFE SAVERS Candy Cane
   Candies
1 yellow LIFE SAVERS Roll Candy
   Royal Frosting (page 43) or prepared white frosting

1. Cut cookie with sharp knife into three pieces as shown (wings should be about ⅜-inch at widest part; body section should be about ½-inch at narrowest part).

2. Attach 2 candy cane roll candies for head, one on top of the other, with frosting. Attach yellow roll candy to head with frosting for halo.

3. Arrange cookie pieces on waxed paper in angel shape (cookies will not touch at this point). With frosting using small star tip, attach wings to angel body, filling in space between body and wings with icing or frosting. Attach head with frosting. Let dry.   *Makes 1 angel*

Holiday Fundamentals

Pastry bags are available in a variety of sizes and materials; they are sold at kitchenware stores and some supermarkets. You can also use a small, resealable plastic food storage bag by snipping ¼ to ½ inch from a corner and inserting a piping tip into the opening. Fill the bag with frosting and seal before using.

Ritz Shining Star

5 Holiday RITZ Crackers
4 red LIFE SAVERS Roll Candies
   Ribbon

1. Arrange crackers side by side in circle so that star shape forms in open center area; set aside.

2. Finely crush candies; evenly spread on foil-lined baking sheet into 2½-inch circle.

3. Bake at 350°F for 4 minutes or until melted. Remove from oven. Immediately press crackers as laid out in step 1 into outer edge of melted candy, pressing firmly to adhere. Cool completely at room temperature.

4. Carefully peel foil from ornament. Using pin or toothpick, enlarge one hole in cracker for ribbon. Thread with ribbon; tie in bow to hang.   *Makes 1 star*

Starlight Wreath

5 FARLEY'S Starlight Mints
10 Chocolate TEDDY GRAHAMS Graham Snacks
   Holiday ribbon, for hanging

1. Place mint candies in circle, alternating with 5 graham snacks on foil-lined baking sheet.

2. Place in 325°F oven for 3 to 4 minutes or until mints are soft and melted. Do not overmelt. Remove from oven and carefully press remaining graham snacks into each melted mint. Cool completely before peeling from foil. Use holiday ribbon for hanging.   *Makes 1 wreath*

Top to bottom:
Ritz Shining Star,
Starlight Wreaths

Best-Loved Desserts ✨

Very Beary Peanut Brittle

   2 cups sugar
   1 cup water
   ½ cup light corn syrup
   1 tablespoon margarine or butter
   ½ cup PLANTERS COCKTAIL Peanuts
   1 teaspoon vanilla extract
   ½ teaspoon baking soda
   1 cup TEDDY GRAHAMS Graham Snacks, any flavor

1. Heat sugar, water, corn syrup and margarine or butter in medium saucepan over medium-low heat, stirring occasionally, until mixture reaches 290°F on candy thermometer.

2. Stir in peanuts; continue to heat to 300°F. Remove from heat; stir in vanilla and baking soda.

3. Thinly spread mixture onto greased baking sheet. Press bear-shaped graham snacks into mixture while still hot.

4. Cool completely; break into bite-size pieces. Store in airtight container for up to 2 weeks.   *Makes about 1½ pounds*

Preparation Time: 15 minutes
Cook Time: 20 minutes
Cooling Time: 2 hours
Total Time: 2 hours and 35 minutes

Very Beary Peanut Brittle

Streusel Coffeecake

32 CHIPS AHOY! Chocolate Chip Cookies, divided
1 (18- to 18.5-ounce) package yellow or white cake mix
½ cup sour cream
½ cup PLANTERS Pecans, chopped
½ cup flaked coconut
¼ cup packed brown sugar
1 teaspoon ground cinnamon
⅓ cup margarine or butter, melted
Powdered sugar glaze, optional

1. Coarsely chop 20 cookies; finely crush remaining 12 cookies. Set aside.

2. Prepare cake mix batter according to package directions; blend in sour cream. Stir in chopped cookies. Pour batter into greased and floured 13×9×2-inch baking pan.

3. Mix cookie crumbs, pecans, coconut, brown sugar and cinnamon; stir in margarine or butter. Sprinkle over cake batter.

4. Bake at 350°F for 40 minutes or until toothpick inserted in center of cake comes out clean. Cool completely. Drizzle with powdered sugar glaze if desired. Cut into squares to serve.

Makes 24 servings

Preparation Time: 25 minutes
Cook Time: 40 minutes
Cooling Time: 2 hours
Total Time: 3 hours and 5 minutes

For more holiday recipes and crafts, visit us at **nabiscorecipes.com.**

Oreo White Chocolate Mousse Cake

1 (1-pound 4-ounce) package Holiday OREO Chocolate
   Sandwich Cookies, divided
6 tablespoons margarine or butter, melted
1 envelope KNOX Unflavored Gelatine
1¼ cups milk, divided
1 (11-ounce) package white chocolate chips
1 pint heavy cream, whipped, or 4 cups prepared
   whipped topping
Fresh raspberries, for garnish

1. Finely crush 24 cookies. Mix crushed cookies and margarine
or butter; press on bottom and 1 inch up side of 9-inch
springform pan. Set aside.

2. Sprinkle gelatine over milk in large saucepan; let stand
1 minute. Stir over low heat about 3 minutes or until gelatine
completely dissolves.

3. Add white chocolate chips to gelatine mixture; continue
heating until chocolate chips are melted and smooth.
Refrigerate 30 minutes or until slightly thickened.

4. Coarsely chop 24 cookies. Gently fold chopped cookies
and whipped cream into cooled chocolate mixture. Spoon into
prepared crust. Refrigerate 6 hours or overnight.

5. Halve remaining cookies; garnish with cookie halves and
raspberries if desired.   *Makes 16 servings*

Preparation Time: 20 minutes
Chill Time: 6 hours and 30 minutes
Total Time: 6 hours and 50 minutes

Oreo White Chocolate
Mousse Cake

Holiday Apple Crisp

**20 HONEY MAID Honey Grahams, finely crushed
   (about 1⅓ cups crumbs)**
⅓ cup margarine or butter, melted
⅓ cup sugar
6 cups coarsely chopped, peeled baking apples
1 cup seedless raisins
1 cup packed light brown sugar
½ cup apple cider
⅓ cup candied lemon peel
2 tablespoons cornstarch
1 teaspoon ground allspice
   Sour Cream Sauce, recipe follows

1. Mix crumbs, margarine or butter and sugar; press half the mixture on bottom of 9×9×2-inch baking dish.

2. Heat apples, raisins, brown sugar, cider, candied lemon peel, cornstarch and allspice in 3-quart saucepan over medium-high heat until mixture boils; reduce heat. Simmer for 10 to 15 minutes, stirring occasionally, until thickened. Spoon over prepared crust; top with remaining crumb mixture.

3. Bake at 375°F for 15 to 20 minutes until topping is browned and fruit mixture is hot and bubbly. Cool slightly. Serve warm with Sour Cream Sauce.   *Makes 10 servings*

Sour Cream Sauce: Blend 1 (8-ounce) container sour cream, ½ cup powdered sugar and 2 tablespoons milk until smooth.

Preparation Time: 15 minutes
Cook Time: 25 minutes
Cooling Time: 10 minutes
Total Time: 50 minutes

Oreo Cookie Bread Pudding

    4 cups day-old French bread or regular bread cubes
    16 OREO Chocolate Sandwich Cookies, coarsely broken
        (about 2 cups cookie pieces)
    2 cups milk
    ½ cup sugar
    ¼ cup margarine or butter, melted
    2 eggs
    1 teaspoon vanilla extract
      Ice cream, optional

1. Mix bread cubes and cookie pieces in large bowl; set aside.

2. Blend milk, sugar, margarine or butter, eggs and vanilla; pour over bread mixture, stirring to coat evenly. Pour into greased 1½-quart round casserole.

3. Bake at 350°F for 45 to 50 minutes or until set. Serve warm or at room temperature topped with ice cream if desired.

Makes 6 servings

Preparation Time: 10 minutes
Cook Time: 45 minutes
Total Time: 55 minutes

For more holiday recipes and crafts, visit us at
nabiscorecipes.com.

Nilla Tiramisu

    2 (8-ounce) packages cream cheese, softened
 ¼ cup powdered sugar
    1 teaspoon vanilla extract
    1 (16-ounce) container frozen whipped topping,
       thawed, divided
  38 NILLA Wafers, divided
 ⅓ cup black coffee
       Chocolate-covered coffee beans and cocoa powder,
       for garnish

1. Beat cream cheese, sugar and vanilla in medium bowl with electric mixer at medium speed until creamy. Stir in 4 cups whipped topping.

2. Spoon ⅓ of cream cheese mixture into 1½-quart serving bowl. Dip 10 wafers in coffee for about 5 seconds and evenly place over cream cheese layer; repeat layers twice. Spread remaining whipped topping over wafers.

3. Refrigerate for at least 1 hour. Garnish with remaining wafers, coffee beans and cocoa powder.   *Makes 8 servings*

Preparation Time: 30 minutes
Chill Time: 1 hour
Total Time: 1 hour and 30 minutes

Oreo Eggnog

    1 quart prepared eggnog
  18 OREO Chocolate Sandwich Cookies, divided
       Prepared whipped topping

1. Blend eggnog and 10 cookies in blender until smooth.

2. Pour into 8 glasses. Serve immediately with whipped topping and remaining cookies.   *Makes 8 servings*

Preparation Time: 10 minutes
Total Time: 10 minutes

Nilla Tiramisu

Reindeer Cupcakes

38 Holiday OREO Chocolate Sandwich Cookies, divided
1 (18.25-ounce) package white cake mix with pudding
1¼ cups water
¼ cup vegetable oil
3 egg whites
48 mini pretzel twists
4 ounces white chocolate, melted
    Red hot candies, white chocolate chips and
        miniature chocolate chips, for decorating
1 (16-ounce) can prepared chocolate frosting

1. Coarsely chop 14 cookies. Mix cake mix, water, oil and
egg whites in large bowl with electric mixer at low speed until
moistened. Beat 2 minutes at high speed. Stir in chopped
cookies. Spoon batter into 24 paper-lined 2½-inch muffin-pan
cups.

2. Bake at 350°F for 20 to 25 minutes or until toothpick
inserted in center comes out clean. Remove from pans; cool
on wire rack.

3. Cut a "V"-shaped portion off each remaining cookie to form
reindeer face. Attach two pretzel twists to cookies using some
melted chocolate for antlers. Decorate face using red hot
candies and chocolate chips. Refrigerate until set.

4. To serve, frost cupcakes with chocolate frosting. Stand
reindeer faces on edge on each cupcake.

Makes 24 cupcakes

Preparation Time: 45 minutes
Cook Time: 20 minutes
Cooling Time: 1 hour
Total Time: 2 hours and 5 minutes

Graham Pecan Toffee

24 squares HONEY MAID Honey Grahams
1 cup sugar
¼ cup margarine or butter
¼ cup water
¼ teaspoon salt
¼ teaspoon baking soda
1 cup PLANTERS Pecans, chopped
3 ounces semisweet chocolate, melted

1. Place crackers on greased 15½×10½×1-inch jelly-roll pan; set aside.

2. Heat sugar, margarine or butter, water and salt in medium saucepan over medium-high heat, stirring constantly until mixture reaches 300°F on candy thermometer (hard-crack stage) or until small amount of mixture dropped into cold water separates into hard, brittle strands. Remove from heat; stir in baking soda.

3. Immediately pour over crackers in pan, spreading evenly. Sprinkle with nuts; cool.

4. Drizzle with melted chocolate. Let stand at room temperature to harden. Break into pieces; store in airtight container

Makes about 1¼ pounds

Preparation Time: 10 minutes
Cook Time: 20 minutes
Cooling Time: 1 hour
Total Time: 1 hour and 30 minutes

For more holiday recipes and crafts, visit us at
nabiscorecipes.com.

Oreo Caramel Clusters

28 FARLEY'S Caramels, unwrapped
1 tablespoon water
60 Mini OREO Bite Size Chocolate Sandwich Cookies
4 ounces semisweet chocolate, melted

1. Heat caramels and water in small saucepan over medium-low heat, stirring until melted and smooth; set aside.

2. Arrange chocolate sandwich cookies in 20 clusters of 3 on waxed paper-lined baking sheet.

3. Spoon 1 teaspoonful caramel mixture over each cookie cluster. Spoon 1 teaspoonful melted chocolate over caramel. Let stand until set. Remove from baking sheet. Store in airtight container. *Makes 20 candies*

Preparation Time: 30 minutes
Cook Time: 10 minutes
Cooling Time: 1 hour
Total Time: 1 hour and 40 minutes

Ritz Bits Bark

2 cups RITZ Bits Peanut Butter Sandwiches
½ cup JET-PUFFED Miniature Marshmallows
⅓ cup PLANTERS COCKTAIL Peanuts
6 (1-ounce) squares semisweet chocolate, melted

1. Mix cracker sandwiches, marshmallows and peanuts in large bowl.

2. Pour melted chocolate over mixture, tossing to coat well. Spread on lightly greased baking sheet.

3. Refrigerate about 30 minutes until chocolate is set. Break into pieces. Store in tightly covered container in refrigerator for up to 1 week. *Makes about ¾ pound*

Preparation Time: 20 minutes
Chill Time: 30 minutes
Total Time: 50 minutes

Pecan Eggnog Cheesecake

¾ cup PLANTERS Pecan Halves, toasted, divided
2 (8-ounce) packages cream cheese, softened
½ cup sugar
2 eggs
⅓ cup sour cream
1 teaspoon rum extract
¾ teaspoon ground nutmeg, divided
1 (9-inch) HONEY MAID Honey Graham Pie Crust
  Prepared whipped topping, for garnish

1. Reserve 8 pecan halves for garnish; finely chop remaining pecans.

2. Beat cream cheese, sugar, eggs, sour cream, rum extract and ½ teaspoon nutmeg in medium bowl with electric mixer until creamy; stir in chopped pecans. Spread into prepared crust.

3. Bake at 350°F for 40 to 45 minutes or until filling is set. Cool completely; refrigerate 3 to 4 hours.

4. Garnish cheesecake with whipped topping, pecan halves and remaining nutmeg.   *Makes 8 servings*

Preparation Time: 20 minutes
Cook Time: 40 minutes
Cooling Time: 1 hour
Chill Time: 3 hours
Total Time: 5 hours

Holiday Classics

Oreo Cheesecake

---

1 (1-pound 4-ounce) package OREO Chocolate
   Sandwich Cookies, divided
⅓ cup margarine or butter, melted
3 (8-ounce) packages cream cheese, softened
¾ cup sugar
4 eggs
1 cup sour cream
1 teaspoon vanilla extract
   Whipped cream and mint sprigs, for garnish
   Additional OREO Chocolate Sandwich Cookies,
      halved, for garnish

1. Finely crush 30 cookies and coarsely chop 20 cookies; set aside. Mix finely crushed cookie crumbs and margarine or butter in bowl. Press on bottom and 2 inches up side of 9-inch springform pan; set aside.

2. Beat cream cheese and sugar in medium bowl with electric mixer at medium speed until creamy. Blend in eggs, sour cream and vanilla; fold in chopped cookies. Spread mixture into prepared crust. Bake at 350°F for 55 to 60 minutes or until set. (If necessary to prevent top from overbrowning, tent with foil for the last 15 to 20 minutes of baking.)

continued on page 70

Oreo Cheesecake

3. Cool on wire rack at room temperature. Refrigerate at least 4 hours.

4. Remove side of pan; garnish with whipped cream, mint sprigs and cookie halves to serve. *Makes 16 servings*

Preparation Time: 25 minutes
Cook Time: 55 minutes
Cooling Time: 1 hour
Chill Time: 4 hours
Total Time: 6 hours and 20 minutes

Mocha Rum Balls

60 NILLA Wafers, finely rolled (about 2½ cups crumbs)
1 cup powdered sugar
1 cup PLANTERS Pecans, finely chopped
½ cup margarine or butter, melted
2 tablespoons light corn syrup
2 tablespoons unsweetened cocoa
¼ cup rum
1 teaspoon instant coffee granules
Powdered sugar, for coating

1. Mix crumbs, 1 cup powdered sugar, pecans, margarine or butter, corn syrup and cocoa in large bowl. Blend rum and instant coffee until coffee granules are dissolved; stir into crumb mixture. Let stand 15 minutes.

2. Shape mixture into 1-inch balls; roll in additional powdered sugar. Store in airtight container, separating layers with waxed paper. Flavor improves with standing.

Makes about 4 dozen

Preparation Time: 40 minutes
Total Time: 40 minutes

Famous Chocolate Refrigerator Roll

1 teaspoon vanilla extract
2 cups heavy cream, whipped, or 1 (8-ounce) container
frozen whipped topping, thawed
1 (9-ounce) package NABISCO Famous Chocolate
Wafers
   Chocolate curls, for garnish

1. Stir vanilla into whipped cream or topping.

2. Spread ½ tablespoon whipped cream or topping on each wafer. Begin stacking wafers together and stand on edge on serving platter to make 14-inch log.

3. Frost with remaining whipped cream or topping. Chill for 4 to 6 hours*. To serve, garnish with chocolate curls; slice roll at 45° angle.   *Makes 12 servings*

*Or, freeze until firm; cover with plastic wrap. Thaw in refrigerator for 1 hour before serving.

Preparation Time: 30 minutes
Chill Time: 4 hours
Total Time: 4 hours and 30 minutes

For more holiday recipes and crafts, visit us at
nabiscorecipes.com.

Ritz Cracker Stuffing

1 cup coarsely chopped mushrooms or broccoli
½ cup chopped onion
½ cup chopped celery
¼ cup margarine or butter
4 Stay Fresh Packs RITZ Crackers, coarsely crushed
  (about 7 cups crumbs)
2 cups PLANTERS Walnuts, Pecans or Almonds,
  coarsely chopped
¼ cup chopped parsley
1 tablespoon poultry seasoning
½ teaspoon ground black pepper
1 (14½-ounce) can chicken broth
2 eggs, beaten

1. Cook mushrooms or broccoli, onion and celery in margarine or butter in skillet over medium heat until tender.

2. Mix cracker crumbs, nuts, parsley, poultry seasoning, pepper and vegetable mixture in large bowl. Add broth and eggs, tossing until well combined. Spoon into 2-quart baking dish or pan; cover.

3. Bake at 325°F for 30 to 40 minutes or until heated through. Or use as stuffing for turkey, chicken or pork.

Makes about 6 cups

Preparation Time: 20 minutes
Cook Time: 35 minutes
Total Time: 55 minutes

Note: For fewer servings, recipe can be halved. Spoon into 1-quart baking dish. Cover; bake at 325°F for 25 to 30 minutes, or microwave at HIGH for 6 to 8 minutes.

Microwave Directions: Combine mushrooms or broccoli, onion, celery and margarine or butter in 2½-quart microwave-proof bowl; cover. Microwave at HIGH (100%) power for 3 to 4 minutes or until tender. Stir in remaining ingredients as above; cover. Microwave at HIGH for 10 to 12 minutes or until hot, stirring after 6 minutes.

Stained Glass Cookies

½ **cup margarine or butter, softened**
½ **cup sugar**
½ **cup honey**
 1 **egg**
 1 **teaspoon vanilla extract**
 3 **cups all-purpose flour**
 1 **teaspoon DAVIS Baking Powder**
½ **teaspoon baking soda**
½ **teaspoon salt**
 5 **(1.14-ounce) rolls LIFE SAVERS Five Flavor Roll
    Candy**

1. Beat margarine or butter, sugar, honey, egg and vanilla in large bowl with electric mixer until creamy. Mix in flour, baking powder, baking soda and salt. Cover; refrigerate at least 2 hours.

2. Roll dough on lightly floured surface to ¼-inch thickness. Cut dough into desired shapes with 2½- to 3-inch floured cookie cutters. Trace smaller version of cookie shape on dough leaving ½- to ¾-inch border of dough. Cut out and remove dough from center of cookies; set aside. Place cut-out shapes on baking sheets lined with foil. Repeat with reserved dough, re-rolling scraps as necessary.

3. Crush each color of candy separately between two layers of wax paper with a mallet. Spoon crushed candy inside centers of cut-out cookie shapes (about ½ teaspoon for each cookie).

4. Bake at 350°F for 6 to 8 minutes or until candy is melted and cookies are lightly browned. Cool cookies completely before removing from foil. *Makes 3½ dozen*

Preparation Time: 1 hour
Chill Time: 2 hours
Cook Time: 6 minutes
Cooling Time: 30 minutes
Total Time: 3 hours and 36 minutes

Stained Glass Cookies

Ritz Mock Apple Pie

    Pastry for two-crust 9-inch pie
 36 **RITZ Crackers, coarsely broken**
        (about 1¾ cups crumbs)
  2 **cups sugar**
1¾ **cups water**
  2 **teaspoons cream of tartar**
  2 **tablespoons lemon juice**
    Grated peel of 1 lemon
  2 **tablespoons margarine or butter**
  ½ **teaspoon ground cinnamon**

1. Roll out half the pastry and line 9-inch pie plate. Place cracker crumbs in prepared crust; set aside.

2. Heat sugar, water and cream of tartar to a boil in saucepan over high heat; simmer for 15 minutes. Add lemon juice and peel; cool.

3. Pour syrup over cracker crumbs. Dot with margarine or butter; sprinkle with cinnamon. Roll out remaining pastry; place over pie. Trim, seal and flute edges. Slit top crust to allow steam to escape.

4. Bake at 425°F for 30 to 35 minutes or until crust is crisp and golden. Cool completely.   *Makes 10 servings*

Preparation Time: 45 minutes
Cook Time: 30 minutes
Cooling Time: 3 hours
Total Time: 4 hours and 15 minutes

Old Fashioned Ice-Box Dessert

15 HONEY MAID Honey Grahams
1 (8-ounce) package cream cheese, softened
3 cups milk
**1 (4-serving size) package ROYAL Instant Vanilla
    Pudding & Pie Filling**
2 cups heavy cream, whipped
⅓ cup flaked coconut, toasted

1. Arrange crackers in even layer on bottom of 13×9×2-inch baking pan; set aside.

2. Beat cream cheese in large bowl with electric mixer until smooth; gradually blend in milk. Add pudding mix; beat for 1 minute. Fold in half the whipped cream.

3. Spread pudding mixture in prepared pan. Spread remaining whipped cream over pudding layer. Refrigerate for at least 2 hours or overnight.

4. Sprinkle with coconut. Cut into squares to serve.

Makes 15 servings

Preparation Time: 25 minutes
Chill Time: 2 hours
Total Time: 2 hours and 25 minutes

*For more holiday recipes and crafts, visit us at
nabiscorecipes.com.*

Velvet Chocolate Cheesecake

30 CHIPS AHOY! Chocolate Chip Cookies, divided
¼ cup margarine or butter, melted
1⅓ cups sugar, divided
2 (8-ounce) packages cream cheese, softened
⅓ cup unsweetened cocoa
2 eggs
1½ teaspoons vanilla extract, divided
1 cup sour cream
Whipped topping and maraschino cherries, for garnish

1. Finely crush 20 cookies. Mix cookie crumbs and margarine or butter; press on bottom of 8-inch springform pan. Stand remaining cookies around side of pan; set aside.

2. Reserve 2 tablespoons sugar. Beat cream cheese in medium bowl with electric mixer at medium speed until creamy; beat in remaining sugar, cocoa, eggs and 1 teaspoon vanilla until fluffy. Pour into prepared crust. Cover tops of cookies with band of aluminum foil before baking to avoid overbrowning.

3. Bake at 375°F for 50 minutes or until cheesecake is puffed and toothpick inserted ½ inch from edge comes out clean; remove from oven.

4. Blend reserved sugar, sour cream and remaining vanilla; spread evenly over cheesecake. Return to oven; bake 10 minutes more. Cool completely at room temperature. Refrigerate for 3 hours or overnight. Remove side of pan. Garnish with whipped topping and maraschino cherries if desired. *Makes 10 servings*

Preparation Time: 20 minutes
Cook Time: 1 hour
Cooling Time: 1 hour
Chill Time: 3 hours
Total Time: 5 hours and 20 minutes

Velvet Chocolate
Cheesecake

Mallow Topped Sweet Potatoes

   3 (15-ounce) cans sweet potatoes, drained
   2 tablespoons margarine or butter, melted
   2 tablespoons orange juice
   2 tablespoons packed brown sugar
   1 teaspoon ground cinnamon
   ¼ teaspoon ground nutmeg
   3 cups JET-PUFFED Marshmallows (about 25)

1. Place sweet potatoes into greased 9×9×2-inch baking pan.

2. Blend margarine or butter, orange juice, brown sugar, cinnamon and nutmeg; pour over potatoes. Bake at 350°F for 15 minutes.

3. Top potatoes with marshmallows. Bake 10 minutes more or until marshmallows are golden brown.   *Makes 8 servings*

Preparation Time: 10 minutes
Cook Time: 25 minutes
Total Time: 35 minutes

Holiday Fundamentals

10 miniature marshmallows = 1 large marshmallow
1 (10-ounce) package contains 40 large marshmallows
1 (10½-ounce) package contains 5½ cups miniature marshmallows

Mallow Topped
Sweet Potatoes

Original Nilla Banana Pudding

¾ **cup sugar, divided**
⅓ **cup all-purpose flour**
   Dash salt
 3 **eggs, separated**
 2 **cups milk**
½ **teaspoon vanilla extract**
45 **NILLA Wafers, divided**
 5 **ripe bananas, sliced (about 3½ cups), divided**
   Additional NILLA Wafers and banana slices, for garnish

1. Mix ½ cup sugar, flour and salt in top of double boiler. Blend in 3 egg yolks and milk. Cook, uncovered, over boiling water, stirring constantly for 10 to 12 minutes or until thickened. Remove from heat; stir in vanilla.

2. Reserve 10 wafers for garnish. Spread small amount of custard on bottom of 1½-quart casserole; cover with layer of wafers and a layer of sliced bananas. Pour about ⅓ of custard over bananas. Continue to layer wafers, bananas and custard to make a total of 3 layers of each, ending with custard.

3. Beat egg whites until soft peaks form; gradually add remaining ¼ cup sugar and beat until stiff but not dry. Spoon on top of pudding, spreading evenly to cover entire surface and sealing well to edges.

4. Bake at 350°F in top half of oven for 15 to 20 minutes or until browned. Cool slightly or refrigerate. Garnish with additional wafers and banana slices just before serving.

Makes 8 servings

Preparation Time: 30 minutes
Cook Time: 15 minutes
Cooling Time: 15 minutes
Total Time: 1 hour

Fantasy Fudge

3 cups sugar
¾ cup margarine or butter
⅔ cup evaporated milk
1 (12-ounce) package semisweet chocolate chips
4 cups JET-PUFFED Miniature Marshmallows
1 cup PLANTERS Walnuts, chopped
1 teaspoon vanilla extract

1. Heat sugar, margarine or butter and milk in large heavy saucepan over medium heat to a boil, stirring constantly.

2. Continue boiling over medium heat 5 minutes or until candy thermometer reaches 234°F, stirring constantly to prevent scorching. Remove from heat.

3. Gradually stir in chocolate chips until melted. Add remaining ingredients; mix well.

4. Pour into greased 9×9×2-inch or 13×9×2-inch pan. Cool at room temperature; cut into squares. Store in airtight container.   *Makes 3 pounds*

Preparation Time: 10 minutes
Cook Time: 15 minutes
Total Time: 25 minutes

Tip: For ease in cutting fudge and cleaning pan, line pan with foil before preparing fudge; lightly grease foil. When fudge has cooled, lift from pan; cut into squares.

Kids in the Kitchen 🎁

Triscuit Cottage

---

4 RITZ Crackers
7 TRISCUIT Wafers
1 can EASY CHEESE Pasteurized Process Cheese
   Spread, any flavor
   Assorted candies and chocolate chips, for
   decorating

1. Place 4 round crackers in square on flat surface. Using 4 square wafers for walls, assemble walls on cracker base, sealing seams with cheese spread.

2. Cut 1 square wafer diagonally in half to form 2 triangles. Use 2 wafer triangles for roof support and 2 remaining square wafers for roof, sealing seams with cheese spread.

3. Outline windows and door with cheese spread; decorate with candies and chocolate chips as desired.

Makes 1 cottage

Preparation Time: 30 minutes
Total Time: 30 minutes

Triscuit Cottage

Santa's Helpers

2 cups *each* **Chocolate, Cinnamon, Honey and Vanilla
    TEDDY GRAHAMS Graham Snacks**
**3 cups LIFE SAVERS GUMMI SAVERS Five Flavor
    Candies**
**1 cup seedless raisins
    FARLEY'S Starlight Mints**
**24 foil bake cups
    Plastic wrap and ribbon**

1. Mix bear-shaped graham snacks, gummi candies, raisins and mints in large bowl.

2. Spoon ½ cup mixture in each bake cup; place each on center of 11½-inch square piece of plastic wrap. Gather up corners, twist together and secure with tape. Tie ribbon around tape. Use as party favors or as tree ornaments.   *Makes 12 cups*

Preparation Time: 30 minutes
Total Time: 30 minutes

Ritz Gobbler

24 RITZ Crackers
 3 ounces cooked turkey pieces
¼ cup jellied or whole berry cranberry sauce

1. Top each cracker with turkey piece and ½ teaspoon cranberry sauce.

2. Serve as an anytime snack.   *Makes 24 snacks*

Preparation Time: 10 minutes
Total Time: 10 minutes

Oreo Hot Cocoa

10 OREO Chocolate Sandwich Cookies, coarsely chopped
3 cups milk
½ cup chocolate-flavored syrup
½ cup JET-PUFFED Miniature Marshmallows

1. Blend chopped cookies, milk and syrup in blender until smooth.

2. Pour into 2-quart saucepan. Heat over medium-high heat, stirring frequently until hot.

3. Ladle into 4 mugs. Top with marshmallows; serve immediately.   *Makes 4 serving.*

Preparation Time: 15 minutes
Cook Time: 5 minutes
Total Time: 20 minutes

Ski Bear Dip

1 cup yogurt or pudding, any flavor
TEDDY GRAHAMS Graham Snacks, any flavor

1. Serve yogurt or pudding as dip with bear-shaped graham snacks.   *Makes about 1 cup*

Preparation Time: 5 minutes
Total Time: 5 minutes

For more holiday recipes and crafts, visit us at **nabiscorecipes.com.**

Crispy Cut-Outs

1 (10-ounce) package JET-PUFFED Marshmallows *or*
    1 (10.5-ounce) package JET-PUFFED Miniature
    Marshmallows
6 cups crisp rice cereal
    Decorator icing, candies and sprinkles, for decorating

1. Place marshmallows in lightly greased large microwavable bowl. Microwave at HIGH (100% power) for 1½ minutes or until melted and smooth, stirring after 45 seconds.

2. Immediately stir in cereal to coat completely; press into greased 15×10×1-inch pan. Let mixture cool 10 minutes. Refrigerate for 1 hour.

3. Cut into assorted holiday shapes with greased holiday-shaped cookie cutters. If desired, use toothpick to make hole at top of cut-out; thread ribbon through hole and tie into bow for hanging. Decorate cut-outs with icings, assorted candies and sprinkles.   *Makes about 1½ dozen cut-outs*

Marshmallow Snowman

1 JET-PUFFED Marshmallow
1 (8-inch) piece ribbon or string
2 SATHER'S Black Gum Drops (large)
    Decorator gels, assorted colors

1. Tie ribbon or string around marshmallow mid-section tightly to separate "head" and "body" section of snowman. Trim ribbon or string if necessary to make scarf.

2. Roll one gum drop flat for the brim of hat; using decorator gel attach remaining gum drop for "bowl" of hat.

3. Make face with decorator gels; use decorator gel to attach hat to snowman's head. Let dry.   *Makes 1 snowman*

Preparation Time: 15 minutes
Total Time: 15 minutes

Top to bottom:
Marshmallow Snowmen
and Crispy Cut-Outs

Graham Greeting Cards

18 whole (5 x 2½-inch) HONEY MAID Honey Grahams
Ribbon or yarn, optional
Decorator icing, any color
Assorted candies, for decorating

1. Place whole graham crackers on clean, flat surface. If desired, attach length of ribbon or yarn to top corners of cracker using icing.

2. Use icing to write holiday greeting on each cracker; decorate with assorted candies. Let dry completely before hanging.

Makes 18 cards

Preparation Time: 30 minutes
Total Time: 30 minutes

Holiday Cookies

Decorator gels and frostings, assorted colors and
flavors
Colored sprinkles and candies
Assorted NABISCO Cookies

1. Use decorator gels, frostings, sprinkles and candies to decorate cookies with holiday scenes.

Preparation Time: 15 minutes
Total Time: 15 minutes

For more holiday recipes and crafts, visit us at
nabiscorecipes.com.

Mallow Popcorn Balls

½ cup margarine or butter
40 JET-PUFFED Marshmallows *or* 4 cups JET-PUFFED
    Miniature Marshmallows
½ teaspoon vanilla extract
¼ teaspoon salt
12 cups popped popcorn

1. Melt margarine or butter in 3-quart saucepan over low heat
Add marshmallows, vanilla and salt; stir until marshmallows
are melted and mixture is smooth.

2. Place popcorn in large bowl; pour marshmallow mixture
over popcorn, mixing lightly to coat.

3. With hands lightly greased, shape mixture into 9 (3-inch)
balls. Place on waxed paper; let stand until firm. Store in
airtight container.   *Makes 9 popcorn balls*

Preparation Time: 30 minutes
Cooling Time: 30 minutes
Total Time: 60 minutes

Microwave Directions: Melt margarine or butter in large
microwavable bowl at HIGH (100% power) for 1 minute. Add
marshmallows, vanilla and salt. Microwave at HIGH for
1½ minutes until melted and smooth, stirring after 45 seconds
Proceed with step 2.

Variations: Add 1 cup of one of the following to the popcorn
mixture: TEDDY GRAHAMS Graham Snacks (any flavor),
LIFE SAVERS GUMMI SAVERS candies, chopped candied
cherries or raisins.

Index

Index

Index

Notes

Notes

METRIC CONVERSION CHART

VOLUME MEASUREMENTS (dry)

1/8 teaspoon = 0.5 mL
1/4 teaspoon = 1 mL
1/2 teaspoon = 2 mL
3/4 teaspoon = 4 mL
1 teaspoon = 5 mL
1 tablespoon = 15 mL
2 tablespoons = 30 mL
1/4 cup = 60 mL
1/3 cup = 75 mL
1/2 cup = 125 mL
2/3 cup = 150 mL
3/4 cup = 175 mL
1 cup = 250 mL
2 cups = 1 pint = 500 mL
3 cups = 750 mL
4 cups = 1 quart = 1 L

VOLUME MEASUREMENTS (fluid)

1 fluid ounce (2 tablespoons) = 30 mL
4 fluid ounces (1/2 cup) = 125 mL
8 fluid ounces (1 cup) = 250 mL
12 fluid ounces (1 1/2 cups) = 375 mL
16 fluid ounces (2 cups) = 500 mL

WEIGHTS (mass)

1/2 ounce = 15 g
1 ounce = 30 g
3 ounces = 90 g
4 ounces = 120 g
8 ounces = 225 g
10 ounces = 285 g
12 ounces = 360 g
16 ounces = 1 pound = 450 g

DIMENSIONS

1/16 inch = 2 mm
1/8 inch = 3 mm
1/4 inch = 6 mm
1/2 inch = 1.5 cm
3/4 inch = 2 cm
1 inch = 2.5 cm

OVEN TEMPERATURES

250°F = 120°C
275°F = 140°C
300°F = 150°C
325°F = 160°C
350°F = 180°C
375°F = 190°C
400°F = 200°C
425°F = 220°C
450°F = 230°C

BAKING PAN SIZES

Utensil	Size in Inches/Quarts	Metric Volume	Size in Centimeters
Baking or Cake Pan (square or rectangular)	8×8×2	2 L	20×20×5
	9×9×2	2.5 L	23×23×5
	12×8×2	3 L	30×20×5
	13×9×2	3.5 L	33×23×5
Loaf Pan	8×4×3	1.5 L	20×10×7
	9×5×3	2 L	23×13×7
Round Layer Cake Pan	8×1½	1.2 L	20×4
	9×1½	1.5 L	23×4
Pie Plate	8×1¼	750 mL	20×3
	9×1¼	1 L	23×3
Baking Dish or Casserole	1 quart	1 L	—
	1½ quart	1.5 L	—
	2 quart	2 L	—